SOUNDS LiKE READING™

BOOK SIX

Whose Shoes Would You Choose?

A LONG VOWEL SOUNDS BOOK WITH CONSONANT DIGRAPHS

Brian P. Cleary

illustrations by

Jason Miskimins

Consultant:

Alice M. Maday

Ph.D. in Early Childhood Education with a Focus in Literacy
Assistant Professor, Retired
Department of Curriculum and Instruction
University of Minnesota

Ⓜ Millbrook Press/Minneapolis

to Miss Mac Ivor,
my fifth-grade teacher in Rocky River, Ohio
—B.P.C.

Millbrook Press
A division of Lerner Publishing Group, Inc.
241 First Avenue North
Minneapolis, MN 55401 U.S.A.

Website address: www.lernerbooks.com

Library of Congress Cataloging-in-Publication Data

Cleary, Brian P., 1959–
     Whose shoes would you choose? : a long vowel sounds book with
consonant digraphs / by Brian P. Cleary ; illustrations by Jason Miskimins ;
consultant: Alice M. Maday.
        p.   cm. — (Sounds like reading)
     ISBN 978–0–8225–7640–2 (lib. bdg. : alk. paper)
     1. English language—Consonants—Juvenile literature. 2. English
language—Vowels—Juvenile literature. 3. Reading—Phonetic method—
Juvenile literature. I. Miskimins, Jason, ill. II. Maday, Alice M. III. Title.
PE1159.C53 2009
428.1'3—dc22   2008012767

Manufactured in the United States of America
1 2 3 4 5 6 – BP – 14 13 12 11 10 09

Dear Parents and Educators,

As a former adult literacy coach and the father of three children, I know that learning to read isn't always easy. That's why I developed **Sounds Like Reading**™—a series that uses a combination of devices to help children learn to read.

This book is the sixth in the **Sounds Like Reading**™ series. It uses rhyme, repetition, illustration, and phonics to introduce young readers to long vowel sounds and consonant digraphs— letter combinations that come together to create a new sound. These include combinations such as *ch*, *sh*, and *th*. I've chosen to use a broad, inclusive definition of digraphs in this book, so you'll also see combinations such as *kn* and *wr*.

Starting on page 4, you'll see three rhyming words on each left-hand page. These words are part of the sentence on the facing page. They all feature long vowels and consonant digraphs. As the book progresses, the sentences become more challenging. These sentences contain a "discovery" word—an extra rhyming word in addition to those that appear on the left. The final sentence in the book contains two discovery words. Children will delight in the increased confidence that finding and decoding these words will bring. They'll also enjoy looking for the mouse that appears throughout the book. The mouse asks readers to look for words that sound alike.

The bridge to literacy is one of the most important we will ever cross. It is my hope that the **Sounds Like Reading**™ series will help young readers to hop, gallop, and skip from one side to the other!

Sincerely,

Brian P. Cleary

Look for me to help you find the words that sound alike!

shone

throne

phone

The sun **shone** on the **throne** as he talked on the **phone**.

each

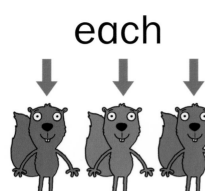

reach

peach

6

Can you find three words that sound alike?

We **each reach** for a **peach**.

she

three

3

knee

Can you find three words that sound alike?

She drew a **three** on her **knee**.

teach

speech

beach

He can **teach** the **speech** at the **beach**.

leech

bleach

screech

EEE!

Can you find three words that sound alike?

The **leech** by the **bleach** made me **screech**.

whose

shoes

choose

Whose shoes should she **choose**?

chief

thief

sheaf

Can you find three words that sound alike?

The **chief** saw the **thief**
with the **sheaf**.

sheik

shriek

EEE!

cheek

EEE!

Can you find three words that sound alike?

The **sheik** will **shriek** if you kiss his **cheek**.

cheese

knees

wheeze

WHEEZE!

Can you find three words that sound alike?

The **cheese** on my **knees** made me **wheeze**.

Mr. Cho

know

throw

Can you find the word that sounds like Mr. Cho, know, and throw?

22

Show Mr. Cho that you **know**
how to **throw**.

Keith

wreath

teeth

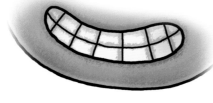

Can you find the word that sounds like Keith, wreath, and teeth?

Keith had a **wreath beneath** his **teeth**.

chew

shoe

threw

Can you find the word that sounds like chew, shoe, and threw?

26

She **knew** she should not **chew**
on the **shoe** that he **threw**.

chose

shows

knows

She **chose those shows** that her friend **knows**.

Ruth

tooth

booth

Can you find two words that sound like Ruth, tooth, and booth?

It is the **truth** that a **youth** named **Ruth** put a **tooth** in the **booth**.

Brian P. Cleary is the author of the best-selling Words Are CATegorical® series as well as the Math Is CATegorical® and Adventures in Memory™ series. He has also written several picture books and poetry books. In addition to his work as a children's author and humorist, Mr. Cleary has been a tutor in an adult literacy program. He lives in Cleveland, Ohio.

Jason Miskimins grew up in Cincinnati, Ohio, and graduated from the Columbus College of Art & Design in 2003. He currently lives in North Olmsted, Ohio, where he works as an illustrator of books and greeting cards.

Alice M. Maday has a master's degree in early childhood education from Butler University in Indianapolis, Indiana, and a Ph.D. in early childhood education, with a focus in literacy, from the University of Minnesota in Minneapolis. Dr. Maday has taught at the college level as well as in elementary schools and preschools throughout the country. In addition, she has served as an emergent literacy educator for kindergarten and first-grade students in Germany for the U.S. Department of Defense. Her research interests include the kindergarten curriculum, emergent literacy, parent and teacher expectations, and the place of preschool in the reading readiness process.

For even more phonics fun, check out all eight SOUNDS LIKE READING™ titles listed on the back of this book!

And find activities, games, and more at www.brianpcleary.com.